# GATHERING OF THE HOMINIDS

# A FAMILY TREE

By

## JACK SHIELDS

ISBN: 1499254849
ISBN 13: 9781499254846

SPECIAL THANKS TO:
Melia Shell, Chris Oleander, & Rupert Fike for help with edit-
ing, Joey Krebs (Phantom Street Artist) for persistence in mov-
ing me forward, & Alex Atman for being here with patience and
understanding
To our children & grandchildren and future generations

Paintings:    Jan Lefler Pg. 48
                  Bliss Morton Pg. 82
Ilustrations: Alex Atman Pg. 65

Editing: Billie Shields
Cover & Back Design Billie Shields
Photograph of rock art used in design     Doak Heyser


For audio spoken word by Jack Shields go to www.reverbnation.

com/jackshields

# IN MEMORY OF JACK SHIELDS
## 1943-2011

### *YOU COME IN DREAM*

*I called to you in dream*
*You came and stood beside me*
*Yet unaware I was there.*
*I called out*
*Begging you to turn*
*One last time*

*Let me touch you*

*I called, and with great effort*
*You were pulled, as if from far away*
*Something remembered from the distant past*
*From deaths shadow to look thru the veil*

*Into your eyes I'm drawn*
*"two black pits direct to the soul"*
*Glowing, psychedelic, a soul wearing a body*
*I feel your kiss upon my mouth*
*Disembodied*
*Wet, alive, light*
*Lingering*
*Yet not sexual*

*A goodbye kiss*
*A holy kiss*

Billie Shields

Jack Shields had a beautiful way of combining his music and words to take us back into our ancient past and collective unconsciousness, the Human Tree... to connect us all to each other, reveal our primal archetypes in the mineral, animal and spiritual being of who we are, living in this space/time present. Let us feel good and learn about our heritage and intelligence to guide us today into a healthy & fruitful future. A pioneer and milestone artist in evolving a poetics rooted in Nature: original, meaningful. If you want to know who and what you are in this place in space, Jack's poetry can help you find your way to the answers.

Chris Oleander/Poet/Teacher/CPITS Poetry Coach

Jack Shields established a life-long poetic language which explored a narrative of explicit portrayals of the human condition through the symbolic motifs of life, birth, death and karma. Jack Shields brought this poetic language to his spoken word through a radical transcendence vis a vis from poetry to performer to radical spoken word poet..

This was the life of Jack Shields and this is his everlasting legacy...

Phantom Street Artist/ Spoken Word Artist

"Jack's poetry combines myth and history to create a modern tribal oral tradition, connecting us with the common roots of our ancestors. ...'Gathering of the Hominids' is brilliant, like a star, one of the absolutely beautiful stars in the late night when workaday consciousness has taken rest and the mind dreams & dreams."

Preston Chase Poet/ (Out & About) Mariposa Gazette

Living in harmony with nature – channeling rhythms of universal connection through pen and voice – is the legacy of poet, Jack Shields. Compassionate free expression and a deep understanding of other realms of coexistence give birth to this amazing body of work.

– Connie Strawbridge, Graphic Designer/Writer

*...We inherit the Earth*
*We the offspring of the ancients*
*We the ancestors of unborn*
*generations*
*We grow up*
*Knowing we're going*
*To end in our graves*
*Knowledge of death*
*Paves the path of the soul*
*No longer eternal,*
*Time enters the mind*
*Sharpens the imagination...*

*Jack Shields "Beyond Dead"*

# INTRODUCTION

The week before Jack died unexpectedly he had told me that his book was finished. I said I'd put it together over the winter so we could have it out the following year. Needless to say, his passing slowed me down. It took almost 2 years before I could start to truly delve into his work. Jack has been brought forth once again as I assemble the pages of this book. This is my memorial to him. His words speak for who he was. He lives forever in my heart and in our children.

In 1984 Jack had a severe accident. While listening for a vacuum leak under our van, it slipped out of park, overran the hand brake. The transaxle of the van caught his head and drug him about 10 feet down the road before a neighbor jumped in and turned it off. His skull was crushed, back broken in 5 places, tissue, ligaments torn. He healed but was left with worsening chronic pain.

Most of these pieces were written after the accident, though a few before. "A Gathering of Hominids: Family Tree"… is our common ancestral history, our bonds, our shared experiences.

Jack's interest was in anthropology, mythology, mysticism… travels of the mind. Many of these pieces were written to be spoken aloud…they live within the voice… the history of time has been marked by the spoken voice more than the written word…. The millenniums around the campfire… voicing the history of the tribe, the storytelling, bringing to life the images. When possible read aloud, find the cadence, rhythm…. The pieces come alive thru the voice…

———

Mine and Jacks grand-daughter, Suki,, who was 10 yr. old at the time, wrote this poem about two weeks after Jack died. It came to her whole as she was drifting to sleep. She said it felt like Jack giving her the poem for me.

*Two are One*
*One is Whole*
*Whole is All*
*All is Everything*
*Everything is Universe*
*Universe is Infinity*
*Infinity is Universe*
*Universe is Everything*
*Everything is All*
*All is Whole*
*Whole is One*
*One is Two*
*Two is two who love*
*One is one who watches over*
*Whole is the amount of soul given to the dead*
*All is all the love they shared*
*Everything is everything they gave to one another*
*Universe is where the dead look upon their loved ones*
*Infinity is the amount of love they hold in their hearts*

*Suki Shields 2011*

# BIOGRAPHY

# BY PHANTOM STREET ARTIST

Jack Shields was born Dec. 26, 1943 in Oakland, Ca. Many stories have been published in the media saying how Jack passed away in his sleep, but he died peacefully sitting in his chair working, doing one of the things he did best, which was representing his son, MMA fighter Jake Shields, as his Manager. Jack was instrumental in his son's MMA career, teaching him the value of hard work and perseverance. Many were profoundly affected by Jack's simple presence in life, sharing sensitivity, compassion and understanding as his virtue.

Jack Shields was a poet, a songwriter, and spirit guide, a devoted father and husband who grew up in Oakland in the early 1940-50's. As a teen, he became interested in the Beat poets of the time. He started taking trips into San Francisco to the City Lights Book store, soaking up all the cultural changes of the times. Poetry, music and the arts were constant companions to Jack.

It was during the heyday of the San Francisco Haight-Ashbury period where Jack first discovered his voice during the counter culture revolution influenced by the Beats. Collectively, the movement prominent in San Francisco complimented and influenced the young ingénue poet who had just completed his military service. After leaving the 101st Airborne Army Infantry with an honorary discharge, Jack began to identify with the great counter cultural movement of the 1960's in writing and performing spoken word prose and narratives. At the end of his life Jack had amassed and produced a prolific body of profound expressed intimations.

In 1970 Jack left San Francisco with a Caravan of brightly painted school buses and vans going across country. It was during this time that he met his wife, Billie. When the Caravan returned to San Francisco, the group decided to buy land together, resulting in Jack and Billie moving to Tennessee on what was called one of the biggest ""Back to the Land" movements in American History. They built a town from the ground up. It became known as "The Farm", a community that started with about 300 people and grew to around 1200 people. The community still exist today with a population of around 200. It was there he started his family. Jack with wife and three sons, Quinn, Clement, and Jake returned to California in 1979, settling in the Sierra Nevada Mountains of Calaveras County.

Over the period of his life, Jack and Billie co-founded several bands including Loco Amor and Planet Pulse. They released several CD's, "In the Garden of the Gods", "Vision Root", & "Earth Mortal Mother". Jack started incorporating spoken word into his songs, later producing a CD of spoken word with music, "Gathering of the Hominids". Around 2000, he became part of American Poets & Writers and he and his wife worked with CPITS (California Poets in the Schools). His work was published in numerous poetry magazines and anthologies.

On the early morning of August 29th, 2011, the world lost a beloved friend, father and mentor, Jack Shields. Jacks poetry and music always echoed the vast depth of his philosophical and spiritual wisdom, which he selflessly shared with all of his relations.

# TABLE OF CONTENTS

Chapter 1 WAY BACK ··············································· 1
AND THE MAN DREAMED: ······························· 2
BECOMING… ·············································· 3
WAY BACK ················································ 5
EARTH MORTAL MOTHER ······························ 8
THIS BEAST ·············································· 10
CREATION MIST ········································· 15
…"BIOLOGY ·············································· 17
FOOD CHAIN ············································ 18
A LONG STORY SHORT ································· 21
GYRUS SUPRAMARGINALIS ··························· 24
--THIRTY THOUSAND YEARS AGO-- ················ 24
*** FIFTEEN THOUSAND YEARS AGO*** ············ 26
NO WONDER, THE WONDER ·························· 27
DIDGERIDOO DREAMS ································· 30
*** MIGRATIONS *** ··································· 33
THE BULL GOD AND HIS BRIDE LIVE IN THE NIGHT SKY ··· 36
ROYAL TOMBS ·········································· 37
BEYOND DEAD ·········································· 41
IN THE GARDEN ········································· 44
WORLDS WEAR AWAY ································· 45

Chapter 2 MYTHIC IMAGINATION ···························· 49
CENTER OF CREATION ································· 50
AUTOGENESIS OF GALAXIES ························ 52
HOLY GHOST GODDESS NO GUILT IN THE GARDEN ······ 54
SHIVA ···················································· 56
GILGAMESH & ENKIDO ································· 58
GHOST BONES ·········································· 63

CLEOPATRA DREAMING · · · · · · · · · · · · · · · · · · · · · · · · · 66
THREE WORLDS WITHOUT FIRE · · · · · · · · · · · · · · · · · 69
AWAY FROM THE WORLD WOMAN · · · · · · · · · · · · · · · 71
CRUSHED & CRUCIFIED · · · · · · · · · · · · · · · · · · · · · · 74
THAT IS ME · · · · · · · · · · · · · · · · · · · · · · · · · · · · · · · 77
LONG HOUSE HOME · · · · · · · · · · · · · · · · · · · · · · · · · 78
ON & ON IT GOES · · · · · · · · · · · · · · · · · · · · · · · · · · · 80

Chapter 3  ENTANGLEMENTS · · · · · · · · · · · · · · · · · · · · 83
HE & SHE · · · · · · · · · · · · · · · · · · · · · · · · · · · · · · · · · 84
THE LEAP · · · · · · · · · · · · · · · · · · · · · · · · · · · · · · · · · 86
ADVENTURE · · · · · · · · · · · · · · · · · · · · · · · · · · · · · · · 86
MYSTERY · · · · · · · · · · · · · · · · · · · · · · · · · · · · · · · · · 87
BATHING IN OUR OWN HOT SPRINGS · · · · · · · · · · · · 89
FROG GODDESS · · · · · · · · · · · · · · · · · · · · · · · · · · · · 91
LIQUID RELAXATION · · · · · · · · · · · · · · · · · · · · · · · · · 91
INTO THE DEPTHS · · · · · · · · · · · · · · · · · · · · · · · · · · 92
TWO-GETHER · · · · · · · · · · · · · · · · · · · · · · · · · · · · · · 94
SOULS · · · · · · · · · · · · · · · · · · · · · · · · · · · · · · · · · · · 96
I DREAMED OF YOU LAST NIGHT · · · · · · · · · · · · · · · 97
RAINSTICK · · · · · · · · · · · · · · · · · · · · · · · · · · · · · · · · 98
I ONLY... · · · · · · · · · · · · · · · · · · · · · · · · · · · · · · · · · 102
YOU DO THAT FOR ME · · · · · · · · · · · · · · · · · · · · · · 103
JUMP FROM ETERNITY · · · · · · · · · · · · · · · · · · · · · · 104


Chapter 4  WALKING ON GIA · · · · · · · · · · · · · · · · · · · · 107
HAWK GLIDES THRU BLUE TIME · · · · · · · · · · · · · · · 108
BUMP ON A STUMP · · · · · · · · · · · · · · · · · · · · · · · · · 111
SPRING MORNING · · · · · · · · · · · · · · · · · · · · · · · · · · 112
MIMOSA MYSTERY'S · · · · · · · · · · · · · · · · · · · · · · · · 114
HIGH MOUNTAIN THICKET · · · · · · · · · · · · · · · · · · · 116
...AND JUST BEYOND THAT · · · · · · · · · · · · · · · · · · · 118
GUST OF SPARROWS · · · · · · · · · · · · · · · · · · · · · · · · 119

TEA LEAVES & OTHER ORACLES · · · · · · · · · · · · · · · · · · · · 120
LOVE FEAST · · · · · · · · · · · · · · · · · · · · · · · · · · · · · · · · 122
IF · · · · · · · · · · · · · · · · · · · · · · · · · · · · · · · · · · · · · · · · · 125
NEW MOON · · · · · · · · · · · · · · · · · · · · · · · · · · · · · · · · · 125
GRIEF IS REAL IS RELEASE IS HEALING · · · · · · · · · · · · · · 127

There are so many worlds in this collection of Jack Shields' poems and spoken-word pieces, some worlds we normally move in and others that we can only access via a visionary passport, what Jack possessed before his untimely death in 2012.

I grew up with Jack, even though we were both in our twenties still growing into men. It is dazzling to read these poems, these reports from what can only be called "the mythic plane," the place where all stories from all tribes are still playing out, the place where our planet is still revered and treated with respect. Many of these poems have musical notations and directions since they were first conceived as song, which is the root of all poetry, as in the first lines we get from Homer when he ask his Muse to "Sing . . ."

There are unexpected turns throughout this book, catches of phrases that startle like this couplet from **Center of Creation,**

*The dead climb up the whirlwind rope*
*to get to the hole in the sky.*

And from **Royal Tombs,**

*There above blue heaven, above the white heaven*
*In the land where the hare hunt happens*

Passages such as these release the reader from the grip of world-weariness that we may not have even been aware we were stuck. The whole of this book takes us to a different place, surely the function and goal of all good art

*Rupert Fike -*

*author of Lotus Buffet (poems), runner-up Georgia Author of the Year, 2011and Voices From The Farm, (non-fiction) accounts of life on a spiritual community in the 1970s*

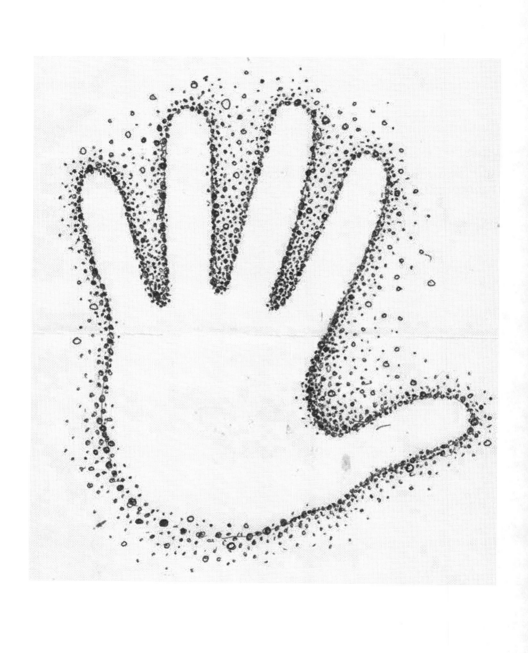

# WAY BACK

*...the past experience revived in the meaning*
*Is not the experience of one life only*
*But of many generations—not forgetting*
*something that is probably quite ineffable:*
*The backward look behind the assurance*
*Of recorded history, the backward half-look*
*Over the shoulder, towards the primitive terror...*
                                                T.S. Eliot

# AND THE MAN DREAMED:

*He was singing a true thing.*

*You are the singer of your life*
*Your heart is the drum beat of your song*

*You live in a home of flesh blood & bone*
*You are singing this thing, this thing*
*You know what this song will bring*

# BECOMING...

Pregnant visions all dreamy like planets
    being born
blown out into past & present now
starlight shifted through green & blue
    cells seize one another
divide, multiply, mate, create
*hereditary traits, stronger wine*
    *blood ties.*
Beyond history, you construct me
    I dissolve in you
memory evaporates in thin air
    prayer breath

Family DNA markers, the mother bones
mitochondria, Sapien Eve
back a hundred thousand years.
    interactive stories
lifetimes develop complexity
computer dog digs swing infinity little bird
    "Rhythm, I entered the flow
    and found it was transformation"

Cuneiform E-mail /cybernetic-cylinder seals/
translated memory/broken-tablets/ Akkadian-clay-pictoglyphs/
origin-orbit/gestation-genius/further-faster/closer-eyes-closed/
direct-contact
my childhood diary hidden under the mattress
these billions of years
appears channeling codes of creation.

Encryption, private language
the secret art of calculation
embroidering clouds weaving words there
    no symbols, no systems
    clouds are poems,
an alphabet of transformation
dream disappear in deep blue
    an information mist seeps thru
    dampens lungs
drips from the ceilings of the skull

Cybernetic garden variety memories
    jump start new desires
    cells thirst saturate
    annihilation & creation

Language is an organism, papillary the one big eye
inchoate, innate unity in thin membranes of memory
    living tissue of time
stuff stored in drawers of blood & flesh
cells that burst into being
    die away
& are replaced each day.

At this still point, drink from the well-spring
the roiling headwaters of chaos & calm
out of the mud & muck & the first worms squirming
    through death

        Dreaming life

        Be-Come from nothing....

# WAY BACK
## (tribal funk, drums, dumbek, guitar, bass, sax)

Memory and imagination, spark creation
The long memory
Mythic imagination
Whole bodies intuitive intelligence
Originating the future now
Creating the creature we become

Biosphere, clouds drift together
Intelligence emerges, language, leaping frogs
Inner & outer worlds intersect
Utterance & understanding
Strategy is strength
From chaos to cosmos
Is to conceive the ground around you
Dark loam, deep root, fruit of family tree
Tell, retell, retain, remember
Cellular memory, multi-cell, single cell
The deep well

Back, Way Back
Before baby booming, fast consuming
Micro-chip information super highway
Before the work week, sound bite speak,
Industrial revolution & pollution
Before kings, queens, cities & states,
Taxman, axe-man, armies and empire
Before herding animals, growing food from the ground,
Farming, settling down

Before Venus figurines, or painting on the walls of caves
Thousands of years before painting on the walls of caves
Filled our graves with traveling gear, food and flowers
Entered the earth, amulet and fetish
In fetal position, faced the sun

In that dawn of the beyond, when the burial bed first led
To another world, out of eternity into time
Burying our dead, carrying their tools
Fire, an old friend thousands of years
Feeling its heat not cooking our meat
Eat our food raw
Paint our faces red
Bury our dead with care
Bear skull sanctuaries
Thighbones through the eyes

Back, way back
Before
Merging, emerging, diverging, evolving, devolving
Unfolding the nautilus and nuclear brainstem
Balanced on the serpent-twined spine
Cellular pandemonium, feathery tamarisk
Family tree, family tree, the long memory

Before Erectus and Neanderthal
Hunt the mammoth
MAMMOTH
With sticks, stones & strategy
Before Habilus, hand hammer, handy man
Before Little Lucy standing up and walking tall
Before primates and mammals

Before trees and seas and life on earth
Before moon and sun
Before the Big Bang
BANG

Before
You were born


In the stillness
Between the beats of the heart
The hammer
About to strike again
Not yet
Not in eternity
Empty

Only by Grace

# EARTH MORTAL MOTHER

Earth
Wheeling, working, creating conditions to support life
Adjusting to maintain temperature and atmosphere
Elements
Fire pulsing thru veins, boiling up from her core
Erupting
Cloud covers, salt seas, cleansing rains
The geology of bones & silky soil

Earth mortal mother, embryo earth, mortal & many sistered
Rounds a middling young sun, our one and faithful life star
This the heart of who we are
Sun rays fishtailing thru a bubbling brew
Of deep dark waters
Boiling, bursting into being
Single cell ceremonies
Spirit spasm, protoplasm
Life-force tossed from chaos sauce
Primordial soup
Amniotic fluids of our planet

The human embryo
Goes through all the stages
Of evolution in the womb
And back
Through the seed & need of every ancestor
Back, way back
Before even life forms,
To Matter…Mother…Ma …
Empty Then

Music of the womb
The soft murmurs of underground streams
The quick pulse of an infants heart
Beating in syncopation
With the slower, stronger, deeper beat
Of the mothers heart
Floods of blood rush through her arteries
Stream through both their veins.

# THIS BEAST
**(acoustic guitars, bass, hand drums)**

This beast you see
can be seized by a song
with eyes for shooting stars
or clouds drifting by the moon
every mothers fruit of the womb
    born to fall and be consumed
    animal of meat, mind, minerals
beast of breastbone morrow, sorrow
breathes moist air, waters dust with
salt-seas-cells-long-memories
you same as me, dust and dew
    grave grasses or
    ashes on the sea

Green grain grass overgrows graves
ash and bones and bones older still
hills of fossils covered clover like
clouds, shrouds, mists
myths blown away
waves, wind is motion
    is mystery
mountains tumble tranquil
trees tremble twisted roots
wrapped round wrinkled rock

and bones and groin-seed
 served up to the sun
 long ago undone
will feed sons and daughters
who in their turn of earth and ash
offer up the roots and worm
 the blessed earth eats

 green, grain grass
 waves over graves

Bones buried with grave gear
covered with pollen of flowers
picked thousands of years gone by

Among the bones known
bones of old people, elders

 someone else
to hunt and forage for them
 crippled in youth
or born with birth defects
yet cared for into old age

From the thousands and thousands
and one nights of tales and ceremony
for man, mammal, survival of the fittest
means something different

Survival of the fittest
something else something other for us
in homes of mammoth tusks
    covered in hides
of rock outcroppings and shallow caves
yawning dark mouth, long rock overhang
just deep enough to make a home
    for fire-making hominids
    or out in the day
tens of thousands of years
in the nights, the stories and stars
the tools of daily life turn on art
sitting round, dancing round fire
wearing the masks and antlers

Men in cool damp dark miles deep
womb of the mother mountain
drinking from the fountain
wellspring of waking dream
down, down, deep along miles
    of dark entrails
to the black belly of the earth
womb of rebirth to manhood
drumming on stalactites, stalagmites
    and ribbons of calcite
pictures of beasts and trancing shamans
    dancing on walls
    torch-lit, shadowy, alive

Man animal emissary, born of both worlds
    the feathered mask
bird face, bird staff, cock stiff
the urge down, down underground
    the soul surge
between twin worlds sliding
crawling out of the birth canal
back among moon and sun


Home hearth, Earth Madonna's
in circled stone altars
feet stuck direct in dirt
    ground of being
Home hearth where woman's magic
birthed and blessed the tribe
where everyone is recognized
Mitochondrial Eve mating
in the dizzying dawn
    long gone
when three races of hominids
    shared the garden
and the serpent's bride joyously
picked the fruits of the tree

Man a million years living
    cold in the dark
    naked no tools

animal hearted love
stone hand ax, chipped flint
Sparks fly
Flaming mind
Fire in the Snow!

The hunt begins at birth
The gathering all within

*We, the acrobats that can raise our own reality*
*Create the creature we become*

# CREATION MIST

Three days working, self illuminated, Elohim created
The heavens & the earth, divided light from darkness
& Earth from water, brought forth grass, seeds, herbs
    & fruit bearing trees…
    On the **fourth day** God made:
*"The two great lights in the firmament of heaven*
*The greater light of day, the lesser light of night"*
How long is a God day, with no concern for moon or sun?
How long between dreams, between Big Bangs
In the vastness of the universe?

    Twelve billion years ago
    Give or take for science sake
    A Brief Burst-a-Big Bang rang
    The bell of beginning.
    6 billion years ago, or so
    A cold dark interstellar cloud collapsed
    Into the swirling disk of fiery gas and dust
    That spawned our solar system.
    The story here, now begins
    Spiral dance & solar winds

    This planet's path in space
    Solar systems as life forms
    As ordinary citizens of
An *almost* empty & endless cosmos
Where pinprick, sunlit bits of life energy
Burst into being and fade away

    Riding the ringed rim, bright Milky Way
    Spiral galaxy, black hole at the core

Matter into energy, back into no matter
Always & ever an equal amount of substance
Flux, Genesis in a fractured vacuum, in a
Crystallized universe of broken symmetry

Life first appears here about a billion years ago
Self-organizing-spontaneous-the-elemental-We
Share intrinsic intimacies with comets & planets
In the poetry of science they say we are "star-stuff"
Born supernova, colliding galaxies, exploding like

THE WORD

*"From the interior of the sky come the songs."*
*"...Godded heart to make things Godded."*

In the beginning, in the spinning cauldron of creation
Gods-goddesses mating, copulating, creating multi-verses
    Space-time warping-curving
-flaring-forth in waves-of -becoming-
    -little-loops-of-conception-

    --Motion the mystery—
"Particles produce rhythmic patterns
        that dance
in dense and subtle form."


    SELF floats emptiness pond
    Dream lotus from navel grows;
        Cosmos

———

## ..."BIOLOGY

is more like history than it is like physics..."


Fitness to survive is a live living process
Dinosaurs lived here for hundreds of millions of years
       then disappeared
The Great Sea Turtles around *long before* the dinosaurs
Witnessed their birth, rise to
       prominence, dominance
       and fall to extinction
Easy come & go with the flow...


In *their* ancient cellular memory
       we a flicker of new life
       hominid come lately
We have pushed them
       to the brink of extinction
We destroy the sea, land and air
Where they have lived
       A quarter of a million millennium


       Microbes and sub-soils
       Percolating dark loam
Critters & processes clean water & air, make oxygen
"The tiny creatures that feed grubs & worms"


       From the bottom up
Need it all or the whole thing falls.
The universe may be expanding
But the earth & it's rare diversity are not

# FOOD CHAIN

(jazz-funk--trap drums, hand percussion, bass, keyboards, guitar, horns)

Living at the top of the food chain
Bragging about the size of our own brain
See the earth, photographed from space
Family tree, tribe, human race

We waste the wealth, recklessly consume
Mammal man, born of mother's womb
Born of the Earth, mortal as we
We destroy the rare diversity
To accumulate money power
Greed the creed it will soon devour
Slow the pace, sake of survival
Face the arrival, an age
Moving fast, fast, fast & faster
Aggressive science, science for profit
A dance with disaster

Our own and only rival for survival
Heavy footin' on the eggshell edge
Death of all dreams, dramas
Fitness to survive, staying alive
Live in an era of hair trigger terror
Where human error
Some fluke, some nuke
Gene turns mean
Bug outsmarts the drug
Fool mistake, all it would take

All the kings horses, all the kings men
Never get it back together again

We don't know what nature knows, we don't know
We don't know what we don't know, we don't know

We this season's seed
Must serve the need
Of every child's trust
Preserve diversity, diversity
One root, one tree, one family
One earth, one tribe, humanity
Diversity, for our tribe to survive
As far to the future as we see to the past
To last as long as say the dinosaur, dinosaur
Can't afford to ignore

Genetically altered food at the store
Ever-deadlier weapons of war
And what's going down
What's going down behind
The corporate doctor's door

Gotta be cool preserve the gene pool
No jacking the genes, no improving the product
Human beings born, ancient mammalian genius
Man's sperm woman's womb
No designer babies custom DNA
Human genes in a Petri dish
Shooting star make a wish
Some fluke, some nuke
Gene turns mean

Fool mistake, all it would take
All the kings horses, all the kings men
Never get it back together again

We don't know what nature knows, we don't know
We don't know what we don't know, we don't know
We don't know what we can't see, what's hidden in mystery
We don't know what nature knows, we don't know

One root, one tree, one family
One earth, one tribe, humanity
Living at the top of the food chain
Bragging about the size of our own brain
See the earth photographed from space
Family tree, tribe, human race

# A LONG STORY SHORT

A billion years
Unfolding-descending backward to original organism
    onward compelled to complexity
    a single cell divides
    grows eyes, nose, fingers, toes

The first primates, monkeys & apes appear a mere
    *36 million years* ago

    Just *five million years* ago
the *first hominids* came down from the trees
where four hands came in handy
down from the disappearing rain forests
to take our first stumbling steps out on the steppes
hunt food on the plains and growing grasslands
    out among the grazing herds.

Less than *three million years ago*
Homo Habilis, our forefather
and uncle to about a dozen dead-end cousins
    picks up stones, crushes bones
    sucks the marrow rich in nutrients
superior new food source, jump-starts brain growth
    fast growing brain, more "found tools"
    more meat, more bones, marrow
grow bigger, stronger, smarter in the hands of Habilis
sticks and stones break bones, names are still unknown.

    Standing upright for line of sight
    a long view good for stalking
    hands free to hold a weapon

feet and legs for walking
run hunt kill with cunning

a *million years ago* we begin to make
a few more contributions to our own evolution
stone hand-axe, use of fire

Evolution in leaps and starts, periods of accelerated
growth for hominids coincide with ice ages;
we grow strong in the cold
Erectus & Neanderthal use fire
develop new tools and weapons
　　the beginnings of ritual & religion

With cunning and curiosity
climb to the top of the food chain

　　-food for thought-
the still hunt, sit silent, alone long hours
…wait for the animal that chooses you…
　　"an empty mind is ready"

& teamwork for the tribe to survive
meat to eat, hides for warmth, bones for tools
drive whole herds to slaughter
　　--the shouts of alarm--
--the groans & grunts of the hunt--

　　Punctuated equilibrium
"to sharpen a stone is to sharpen the mind"
　　---to make a tool for making tools---
　　A new moment of primate mutation

A thousand millenniums
herky, jerky changes until…
      Suddenly
       about
*sixty thousand years* ago we begin
to permute our own transformation
imagination & manifestation, conception & creation
exponentially faster modifications incredible in nature
exuding language, tools, art, culture and religion
-- a blink between binocular bipedal primates
    & human consciousness—

# GYRUS SUPRAMARGINALIS

Speak with given voice, words rain soak thru
words breathe fill up & empty the minds eye
the voice leaves no choice, words come swarming
the meaning, the sounds, swelling understanding
call things out, make them real…

> -words are connections-
> ideation *is* creation
> *the thought itself*
> to have an inner voice
> is to have vocabulary
> not just to express an idea
> but to *formulate* it.

> *"Words are not the end of thought*
> *they are where it begins"*

———

# --THIRTY THOUSAND

# YEARS AGO--

With art comes the goddess
Ivory & mammoth bone Madonna's
Elegant female Venus figurines
Focus on fertility
Featureless faces, no feet
Pendulous breast, large hips
Exaggerated vulva V

& vulvas carved & painted with red ochre
Incised at the entrance/exit
Of the deep cathedral caves

Larva labyrinth, death cocoon
Serpent of rebirth, bird of soul flight
The lunar crescent, Horns of the moon,
*All belong to the goddess of the great hunt*
Long before...
Her bison horn, horn of thirteen stripes
Pregnancy stick, & lunar calendar
One hand lifts her crescent to the moon
      The other rests on her womb
Thirteen months in the lunar year
Thirteen days between the new moon & the full
Thirteen days between menstruation & ovulation

Thirty thousand years of spiritual & economic stability
      Of the healing hearth & temple caves
            Woman's magic round the fire
                  Hot food, healing herbs
She transforms water & meat into blood
Into babies, into milk for babies
Her body magic abundant as the earth

Men's magic, wooden & bone flutes
Draw on walls deep in the earth
Give birth to new herds.
Tools as art
Art as science
Atlatel & bow

Dogs join the hunt

# *** FIFTEEN THOUSAND YEARS AGO***

*The Moon-Bull becomes the Bull of the Herd*

*Hunters become herders*
*Millenniums follow the herds--stay close*
*Keep track of where, when, then someone*
*Somewhere turns the migration back*
*Leads the herd to green pastures of their choice*
*Years of observation*
*Learn bull-heifer relationship*
*Separate calves*
*Pull the young bulls, begin breeding*

*Long before they were domesticated*
*Cattle equaled meat, milk and visionary mushrooms*
*Many magic mushrooms*
*Grow only in the dung of cattle*
*Trailing herds through savannah's and grasslands*
*Where foraging is sparse, but*
*Psycho-active mushrooms cover the ground year round*

# NO WONDER, THE WONDER

Psilocybe cubensis
"Produces feelings of bewitching novelty
    ecstatic experience"
Stimulates imagination & consciousness
--small dose increases visual acuity--
--is sensual inspires sex/procreation--
Higher doses jolt the projective imagination
    Expand consciousness
    --Dance-song-language--
    --a sense of playfulness--
    adaptive advantages

For millenniums savannah's & grassland
Surround the Tassili Plateau in North Africa
    A vast windswept wasteland
    Endless canyons
    Tall perpendicular stone escarpments

Down coiled corridors, thru narrow passages
Often touching wrinkled rock
White or ruddy red windblown sandstone
Dark brown lava rock, tufts of pink
    The ancient skin rough & cool

    In the shadows of the canyon
    Long dark vertical crevices
    Craggy clefts, fissures
    Corridors, caves
    A labyrinth of russet alleyways

Scattered to the four directions
Some lead to thirst, desolation
Long dead river beds...

The power path circles inward to secret springs
Wells, mirages and real human miracles
       At the center of the maze
Amazing paintings first appear 20,000 years ago
Rendered in charcoal & red ochre
On monolithic walls of mother-rock

Surreal pictures of bee headed shamans
       Fists full of mushrooms
Mushrooms sprout out of the body

The body covered by geometric designs
       Like the inside of a beehive
And all around surrounded by visions
Mushroom headed people dancing

Realistic renditions of large herds
       Of long horned cattle
Of the "Great Horned Goddess"
Her arms stretch out and up
Like the horns on her head
She whirls, dances in ecstasy
Her kindred kind everywhere
       Fill the air with
Unintelligible dreams & visions

The mind slipping gears
Double-clutching itself into new realms

Of risk and terror to ecstasy and wisdom
The vision-voyage begins within
   -world without end-
Fasting, breathing, drumming, humming
The beehive mind finds its need
   And feeds it

# DIDGERIDOO DREAMS

(tribal funk-- traps, congas, bass, mandolin, didgeridoo, hand percussion)

*We don't know what dreams are*
  *what dreams are*
Are they real, can they heal?
Didgeridoo dreams raining frogs out of the earth
Bullroaring didgeridoo, druid drone, didgeridoo
Blue moan, see thru taboo
Tattoo you, tattoo you on my soul
Sow the seeds, see them grow
Druid drone, buzz of bee
  *Floods of honey flow*

Beneath the broken moon's sea of tranquility
Libraries of drifting sands
The single body of beauty and the beast
  Enuff is Enuff plenty is all we need
  Only the ghost we feed become flesh
  Let one ghost only pierce and enter
Center in your soul, sing in your dreams
Let your inner ear open to the clear tone
  Own hearts drum
  Own hearts drum

*Hum, humming hummingbird*
*Sing with your wings little shaman*
*Dance, flight, song are one*
  *Hum*

Enlightened, endarkened,
inner-wilderness, animal mysteries
 Commonality of creatures
 Commonality of creatures
Ecology of soul and living planet entwined
 Meat, mother of mind
And meat the mystery of emptiness

Embryo of the earth, infant, elder of the tribe
 Bright as moon or sun
 Dark as womb or grave
 Crave nothing
 Save nothing
 Burn like a good fire

Seasons surrender, the ticking stars turn
Learn to live mostly as mammal
Immortal moment, eternal in time

I'm talking working man's mystical
What works, what matters, materializes
What you manifest, make real
Heart heal, mind mend, time trance
Bones magic, bare bones

External soul, inner organs transparent
Pierced heart opens, the rose encircled heart
Mad blood beating, thorn prick and budding dove
Solitude, vision quest, plant hallucinogens
 animal dance, trance, entrance
 animal dance, trance, entrance
Mimes, magic, mystical imagination

Walls weeping, sweating, ceiling dripping
Milk of knosis, tears of the toad
Didgeridoo dreams
Raining frogs out of the earth
    Bullroaring didgeridoo
Druid drone didgeridoo
Blue moan see thru taboo
Tattoo you, tattoo you on my soul
Sow the seeds see them grow

*We don't know what dreams are*
    *What dreams are*
*Are they're real, can they heal*
    *Didgeridoo dreams*
Sweat cleanses the flesh
Gratitude cleanses the soul
Forgiveness make whole
Druid drone, buzz of bee
    Floods of honey
    Floods of honey flow

*Hum, humming hummingbird*
*Sing with your wings little shaman*
*Dance, flight, song are one*
    *Hum*

# *** MIGRATIONS ***

Many migrations for the far ranging cattle wranglers
*15 thousand years ago,* into pre-dynastic Egypt
Hathor with cow horns, daughter & wandering eye of RA
*12 thousand years ago,* to Palestine & on to
The Fertile Crescent, Persia & India
    Rock art Sahara-Sudanese ware
    Shrines feature bulls in bas-relief
    & mushroom-headed Sin spins in
The long shadow of the Horned Goddess

The cattle wranglers with their mushroom shamans
& collective-euphoric-dance-trance-visionary-culture
Develop early Neolithic villages and towns
That prosper and grow for thousands of years
Become cities, --cities without walls--
Develop deep shamanic-yogic-goddess
Connected spiritual traditions
Cattle are part of art & ceremony
    & songs are of SOMA
*"thy exhilarating all pervading juices*
    *Herb of Light—swift as thought"*

From foraging to farming
"Food sprouts in compost heap
The mind leaps, sees seed as source"

Along the river valleys old tribal *campsites & power spots*
Become *villages,* develop farming, discover irrigation
    Build silos, corrals

More food year round, *village* becomes *town*
Men wear elaborate penis sheaths
Sandals & feathers in their hair
Women wear woven skirts
Decorated in plant dyes, geometric designs

Farmers, fishers, potters, builders, weavers
Build papyrus bundle boats, begin to trade
*Towns* become *cities*, become *city-states*

In the fertile crescent
The bull of the north
Meets and merges with
Serpent of the south


When the horse & chariot tribes of the Steppes
Entered the Fertile Crescent & India
They discovered rich Neolithic cultures
Cities without walls, without a god of war
Easy prey, but they are soon overcome by
The more imaginative cultural & spiritual beliefs
Of the native peoples
Buttressed by the euphoric sacraments of
      SOMA
The War God weds the Ancient Goddess
And is tempered in Her heat

The old ways; hunter-gatherers
Animal dance, mimes, magic, power spots
Shaman, trance, entrance
Strong individuals, self reliance

As hunting gives way to herding
As gathering gives way to gardening
Water and weather patterns
Ritual sacrifice and the sacrifice of seed

Priesthoods thrive, stories & stars
Long centuries watching the skies
Able to predict solar & lunar eclipse
Comets & meteor showers

Priest *increase their powers*

# THE BULL GOD AND HIS BRIDE
# LIVE IN THE NIGHT SKY

Where their comings and goings
Are as predictable as the sunrise
The mathematics of the moon and sun
The visible planets and constellations
Knowledge accumulated long before writing, passed down
By rhythmic repetition, metered memory, the oral tradition

From painted caves & petroglyphs to cuneiform and
hieroglyphics
From tribe and community to worker bee and hierarchy
"History is born with the written word
Is born full brim"
A million years of memory precede cuneiform writing
Wedges to count cattle, stored grain
Walls to protect accumulated wealth
Wars to increase wealth
Gates & guards, taxman, axe-man
Slaves & forced labor
Time clocks & parking meters

**5,000 years ago *Moon-Bull becomes the Bull of the Herd***

# ROYAL TOMBS

We build ziggurat mountains
To touch God
To watch the sky
To measure time
To mark the four corners of the solar year
*The comings and goings of the shadow shedding moon*
*The serpent moon, old man moon wears the horns of the bull*
*Moon maiden, moves women, tides, timber wolves*
*Moon mother grows full and old*
Dies, is reborn to light the skies

In the beginning of civilizations as hierarchy peaks

When death comes for the king
Absolute power does its
Absolute thing…

In the shadows of ziggurats
In the royal tombs of Ur
God-kings buried with their entire courts
To the music of bull-bearded harps
Heads & horns of hammered gold
Beards of lapis lazuli

Councilors, musicians, cooks and concubines
All dressed in regal robes
All interred alive, with their deceased lord
    *A-Bar-Gi*

All to be reborn, eternal as the moon
Always the death following girls
    Sixty eight female skeletons
Red robes, green eye shadow
    Golden bows, silver bows
    All laid out in equal rows
    Laid down alive to drink
    Death from the God cup
To be reborn among the stars

*When the moon sets, Venus follows*


Queen *Shub-Ad, Her* entire court
Buried in a gown of tiny beads, thousands of tiny beads
Of gold, silver, lapis, cornelian, agate, & chalcedony
On her diadem, herds of golden animals run on a field of blue
lapis
Bulls, stags, goats, & gazelles separated by rosettes and
pomegranates
    *By her hand the golden cup of her setting star*

*In Egypt*
In the shadows of pyramids, tombs beyond time
Where Pharaohs travel with trusted retainers
Sail the soul's boat to the land of their fathers
Where hearts are weighed against a feather

And the weight of gold is the flesh of Ra
   Embalmed, mummified, immortal
     *The ritually buried are gods*

*In Europe*
In the shadows of monoliths and megaliths
Huge rock slabs surround burial mounds
Barrows & kurgans where Kings are accompanied
By wives, concubines, servants & soldiers
Bodies covered in red ochre
And horses, hundreds of horses
Whole herds of horses

The mother bones, the old bones
      The single tribe
Born of the bones of our ancestors
Who used the saliva of fighting bears
To stimulate the fermentation of beer
Made the horse sacrifice
Climb the thunderstruck oak
Climb to the land where the three ladders lead
Climb the rungs at ladders end, read the runes
There above blue heaven, above white heaven
In the land where the hare hunt happens
*Come to speak with the one*
*Whom the moons axe edge spares*

*In the Americas*
In Chaco Canyon
One male, 13 female skeletons, resin of cedar and sage
In the shadow of Cahokia, among the Mississippian mounds
Rebirth into the womb of the Earth
A man buried on a bed of beads

On thousands of beads
Spread into the shape of a great bird
57 female skeletons

In the Jaguar temples & pyramids
Of the Mayans & Aztecs
On the stairway of skulls & snakes
In the Codices, bird-song, picture-poems, flower-poems,
Black-flower-of-the-night-sky, Red-flower-of-the-day
The flayed god wears the skin of a virgin
*And the bloody mask of the sun asks for a beating heart*

*In China*
One hundred and two bronze bells
Each the moon and sun
Twenty one female skeletons
Lacquer from the sap of sumac trees
Bells across the divide
The ancestors need music
Drink drums, breathe bells
The bell that broke the lightning bolt
Spoke its spells in spirit voices

*We don't live beyond dreams*
*Want beyond dead*
*Want beyond kings*
*Want to be Gods*
*Want to stop time*
*Want eternal*
*Want forever*
*Want to take IT with us*

# BEYOND DEAD

*We don't know what dreams are*
*What dreams are*
Thats what I said, I said *we don't know*
*What we don't know is what we fear*
She said, *isn't it clear*
*Fear of the unknown*
*The bone of contention*
*Never mentioned*
*The skeleton in the closet is dead*
That's what she said
*No rest in rigid conformity*
*The buried from their bed*
*The awake shake free*
*And dream...*

We inherit the Earth
We the offspring of the ancients
We the ancestors of unborn generations
We grow up knowing we're going
To end in our graves
Knowledge of death
Paves the path of the soul
No longer eternal, time enters the mind
Sharpens the imagination

Wanting a happy hunting ground
Hunting for a happy hereafter
Wanting beyond dead
Is how we got to who we are

Burial gear
First sign of symbolic thought
Religion, science, art start here
Where the heart of death sounds silently
      Startles we to attention,
      Pulls the many tentacles
      Of far flung thought together
      Tethers mind tight to heart


      Waste no part of the animal
      No part of the plant
      With the sacrifice of seed
      Death and decay lead to rebirth
      "We this seasons seed"
      Need the long memory
      Mythic imagination

Day of the Dead
Catholic funeral, bagpipes of pagan Pan
All night picnic in the village graveyard
      The dead participate in life
      The living enriched by eternity
We want to hold our dead
      Want to let them go
Spread our blankets with food & wine
Introduce new babies, husbands, wives
      News for the dead
Share the daily bread of our lives
      We their seed, their progeny
      They substance of our souls
      Dance in our DNA

Make them welcome they visit your dreams

We don't live beyond dream
	Beyond kings

		Want to stop time
		Want eternal
		Want forever
		Want to take IT with us

*All we take to the grave*
*Is the life we've led, the love we gave*
*The life we live, the love we give*

*We all want beyond dead*
That's what she said
*No rest in rigid conformity*
*The buried from their bed*
*The awake shake free*
	*And dream*

# IN THE GARDEN

In the garden with all our restless relatives
all beings that move on the earth
dark earth of our birth
great mothering earth will die
as sure as I and I in time's long place
the long clocks tick and toll time-space
this place, planet, changing season
       passing generation

       In this moment
this beast is released in sudden seizure
       the summoned soul
       consumed whole
       awake aware
       share the single eye
connect, reconnect, wisdom, now knowledge

    Ancient in our souls & cells
       Self-preservation
   the whole self
      beyond dead
   & passing generations

# WORLDS WEAR AWAY

*(jazz-rock)*

Wounded wail of the last dinosaur
Worlds wear away as waves wash the shore
The radio roars, the humming horn soars
Drowned in drunken drums keeping time
The many masks' hand made, worn, torn
Washed away by the tides
And the tides beat against the beach
Beating out time in eternity
Born, buried again
In a rhythm of silent stars
Keeping time

There in the cities,
Where pillars of gray and black smoke hold off the sky
The metallic breath of the worm driven machinery
The whirring and whining wires
Kilowatt-hours, bartered days, lost nights
No return minutes
Real memory can't replace space
Time is all we have to spend
ALL we have to spend
Waste no space trying to avoid
The VOID

NOT to step on the treadmill
NOT to march to the goose-step beat

NOT to walk to the tick of the clock
NOT to turn back pillar of salt
Not a world of man driven machines
More a world of machine driven men
Mad monotony, ruinous routine
Time divided exactly
Hours,      days,   weeks,        years
A lifetime driven by mechanical clocks
To endless repetitive labor
Never a *truly free* moment
Never naked     N O W
But always
Just a few ticks


Between

    Where you've been

        And where

            You must go

Crucified on our own cleverness
Driven to inhabit the clockworks of
T i c k i n g        t i m e

Rock dropped as matter
Clocked in time

BIG        BOOM        BANG

An expanding universe
Everything moves farther and farther a p a  r      t
Boomerang
It all draws back together

Inhale

Exhale

This moment
Immediate
Immense
Blink & Gone
Walking on

Wounded wail of the last dinosaur
Worlds wear away as waves wash the shore
The radio roars, the humming horn soars
Drowned in drunken drums keeping time
The many mask, hand made, worn, torn
Washed away by the tides
And the tides beat against the beach
Beating out time in eternity
Born, buried again
In a rhythm of silent stars
Keeping time

          Keeping time

                    Keeping time

# MYTHIC IMAGINATION

**NO MATTER, NEVER MIND**

*The father is the Void*
*The Wife  Waves*

*Their child is Matter.*

*Matter makes it with his mother*
*And their child is Life*
*        A daughter*

*The Daughter is the Great Mother*
*Who with her father/brother Matter*
*        As her lover*

*Gives birth to the Mind*


**GARY SNYDER**

# CENTER OF CREATION

The dead climb up the whirlwind rope
To get to the hole in the sky
Where sharp tongues of blue obsidian
Sing healing songs
And medicine midwife delivers them
To their new mother

Billowy clouds open and part
Their pearly gates
Tall sun following flowers
Shudder and shower golden pollen
On each of the dead
Who climb the whirlwind

For each a petal falls
Damp with dew
Decays in beauty
Becomes part of the earth
Monument more perfect and permanent
Than pyramids

And for those willing to risk
Resurrection
They sail silent, rudderless
On blue black waves to the glass castle
To rest on the revolving bed where she
Shatters dreams

All awake!
She scatters dreams
She cast the first stone onto the
Pond of concentric circles

At the Center of creation

# AUTOGENESIS OF GALAXIES

Nebulous, Mother of suns,
Seething cloud at the center
Numinous, Mother of sons,
Madonna of sexual birth
Mud-mother of the
Damp-seeded earth & fruit bearing tree

The biology of the Gods
In the geology of the rugged earth
The mystical unbounded
Imagination of its creatures

The auto-genesis of galaxies
The self-articulation of stars
The spontaneity of mountain ranges
Living in a spiral galaxy
One of many billions
Billiard balls and butterflies
Bonded to distant galaxies
Wedded in the womb of gravity

Particles pulse in space
          Vast
Gone beyond imagination
Galaxies beyond galaxies
Of wheeling stars
Become-grow-die-decompose
Flare-forth-come-together-again
          Or
Galaxies within galaxies

Spinning atoms
In subatomic worlds beneath
Our microscopic vision

Out of the background radiation
Of an expanding Universe
The mathematics
Of sculptured creation
Out of the worn world's womb
The tangled birth
Of love and falling leaves

Out of the great mystery holding us
And holding us together
The binding forces embracing atoms
And solar systems

No basic building block
No fundamental particle
Every particle related to every other
In actual mystery waves
Of spiritual scientific reality

The self-articulation of stars
The auto-genesis of galaxies
The spontaneity of mountain ranges

Wash fuzz off a peach
With a garden hose
Eat the peach    bury the pit

# HOLY GHOST GODDESS

# NO GUILT IN THE GARDEN

There where goat-footed men
And green girls dance and sing
She sings, she brings bundles of wheat
Clusters of red & green grapes
Bathes in cedar & sage, covers herself
With charcoal soot and pine resin
Scrawls a labyrinth from navel down
And around her vulva V
Entrance, exit, void, vortex
No heads without tails
No empty shadows, full-fed phantoms
Soulful antique nutrients
Soil, seed, umbilical root & fruit of the Blackbird Tree
Where greenwood druids oaken prayer hangs on holly
& sea spray.

Holy-Ghost-given-goddess-new-life-midwife
Hangs down Heaven's hair
Rapunzel's rope, green hope living sap
The navel string we climb
To the boar tusk labyrinth of the mind
Where spider weaves and leaves a cat's cradle map
Geography-of-death-landscape-of-life
Reflected in smoking mirrors
Where the earth-obsessed moon
Pulls on the mind's tides
In-Sea-sucking-synogue-swirls
Redemptions-waters-waves-break-on-land-

Baptized in semen & salt wind we *begin now,*
Under shifting lunar shadows twine serpents shed their skin,
*begin new*
*Snake swallows tail, figure eights on infinity ice*

Holy Ghost goddess
Earth maker's mother walks in old groves
Where bare feet awake snake awake
As soon as made footfalls fade, loosing spirits of the land
Every blade of grass greener, every green wood spirit keener
Goddess-God/no gender/all gender/all generating/
One whole & holy source of creation
For every hunger & need there is soil & seed

Resist not evil, in darkness shine
What you want is what you get most of the time
Loosen the tight jaw of judgment
Lest you lose perspective
To calm winds, to ease anger
Relax your wings and sing
The great mystery is not a problem
Walk in miracles, drink deeply at mirages
Disappear in mist
*Holy Spirit is the Goddess*
*The Goddess Gift, no guilt in the garden*

### Forty five hundred years ago

## SHIVA

Shiva, Kali, Devi, Shakti,
Lingum, yoni, yoga, union
Shiva ever erect, never sheds his semen

Shiva old man, Shiva ancient among gods
Shiva of skulls, of the moon, of time, of eternity
Dances in a ring of fire, each step of the dance
    birth   death  re-birth
Shiva, pure white lord of the lotus, lord of sleep
And Great Snake, jet black Kundulini
Devi, sleeps coiled at the core
At the base of the spinal column
Ascends only when aroused
Aroused, she rises, pierces the seven centers
Awakens the snake curled below the groin

Kali, black Kali, Shakti, Devi, all embracing female power
Yoni, feminine chalice, cup of creation
Smokey veiled visions, vermillion henna sunsets
Bliss hibiscus    kangaroo womb
Wingwise mantra MA

Through grief curtains of bliss
Kiss Kali's fingers    tear her toes
She dances in fire    dances on hot coals
Dances with the Vajra sword
Cuts like a blade of grass the slice of melting ice
Kali, black Kali, dances to bone trumpets and whistles

Vulva cave, hollow eyed voice, aware of silence
Weather beaten and windy, deep music
The beating bones, the ticks & turns of time
Human skull drums      Kali
Naked, a necklace of polished candle-eyed skulls
A short skirt of human arms

Shiva      Shakti Yoga  Union
Shiva millenniums in the lotus of erection
Shiva, the old shaman, awakened by the arrow
Shiva of four arms, of three eyes, cobra crowned
Shiva, Shakti two are one

Seed of the sun


Kali, jet black Kali
At death She in her terrible aspect
Kohl-eyed, snaked-braided Medusa
She appears as your own fears
Face & embrace her
Night embraces day
New life from decay

Beneath dancing feet
She grinds the dead to dust
Binds the bones of phantoms
Fear and nightmare
From Her dark womb
Rebirth in light

# GILGAMESH & ENKIDO

The neophyte moon, born again chrysalis & cocoon
As wind-well weathers blow blossoms of mandrake shape
Crescent brow knotted in thought
The holy head caught glimpse
The ghastly fear by crackling fire
Ghostly dark does spark

Knaves dig graves
For those who swagger to the crack
& turn their back to better see
What's left for them to lift
Dust settles heavy on the sea
Cracking snapping doom & damned if
I will or won't bend a knee for bells that toll
The crevasse of today's death.

I, *Gilgamesh*, king of the four cornered universe
Lion lifter of Uruk, built my walls of baked brick
Built them twenty feet tall, eight feet thick
The great gates swing at my command
Fight I to expand my land and domain
In every direction pillars proclaim my fame

Every conquest an erection
I rut & root day & night
Women my delight, my weakness
Virgins, sacred whores & warriors' wives
In love & friendship never wise

Made a mess, yes & confess:
It was all wrong
The blame belongs to me
Should have let Great Enkido be.

Enkido, the wild man that ran with lions & leopards
He was a wilderness that could not be tamed
Until I sent woman;
Vestal-virgin-priestess-prostitute
Shambat was all that.

*I, Enkido, no woman had I ever seen*
*Until Shambat came as from a dream*
*She knew my desires set dark*
*Yet watered me in seeded sex*
*Standing on toe tips*
*To kiss with heart-shaped-red-lips*
*Her neophyte nipples rosy as first light*

*Shambat, all abandon, knew no halfhearted ways*
*"For six days & seven nights our lovemaking shook the earth"*
*The pleasure bird sings sweeter in the wild land*
*Beyond all sight of skyward towers, beyond all walls & fences*
*In the beginning of green seeded gardens when*
*All tilled and labored land was called Paradise*
*The untamed world where wild things ran known as Eden.*
*The last Adam falling rising to the occasion*

Enkido came, was spent; lay awake
Full of joy until she awoke & spoke no words

A short embrace, a final kiss
Stroked his face, turned, headed home
& for the first time he felt alone
Wild beast no longer joined his feast
But stayed far away

Until the day
He came to live among men
And became my one friend
We spent our days & nights
Wrestling, running, rambling round
I taught him gambling
We got in fights, went with women
Waged war, easily defeating every enemy

Until that day in my pride
I bade him ride against the Bull of Heaven
The goddess of our city set free the Bull
As a warning to *me*
Enkido said no, he would stay away
And begged me to bend my knee

But I goaded the Great Bull
He beat his hoofs against the ground
And with frenzied attack wore me down
The end was near and to my shame I felt fear
Then my friend Enkido
Took the Bull by the horns
& held him still, until I could strike & kill.

The thrill
The Bulls horn
Torn, flesh and bellow
Tentacle and terror
Take the power
Of mud and blood
Unto myself

Then the mountains bearing Enkido
Shook to their foundations
He fell sick and shortly died

His death sent me wheeling
Crying dying inside
I launched that long tangled search
For life ever-after
And the Old Man & his Wife
Oldest & wind & water wise
Who saved all living beings
From the world flood
Sent my blood pounding
Showed me that spot
Where the plant of eternal life
Lived below the waves
At the bottom of the Ocean Sea

I dived many times to exhaustion
Bringing the plant to shore
My heart soared & I roared like the wild man
        Ran to clear water, running stream
        Drank & slept without dream

Snake took plant
Sliding deep into earth
　　　Ate eternal life

　　　Awake I cried
　　　Later learned to live & die

　　　The natural death.

# GHOST BONES
(congas, hand percussion, guitar, bass, shakuhachi)

*Holy ghost gods and goddesses*
*come before your eyes*
*the old gods long gone*
*glad to see you again*
*glad to see you*
*The ghost bones call*

No control over the dead in the dark of day
Or prayer by the cobweb covered bones in the skeletal crypt
Not even ownership of dust and dew.
Whose spirit sails at the helm of that burning grave
Floats out to sea and sinks
Whose spirit at the helm of that burning grave?

You are the child set adrift in a reed boat
In an ark of osier and sedge
On a river of rocks rapture
      The sheer drop certain death
      Out of the matrix of the mother
      Lifted from her lap
      Folded in her arms
      Lips turn to her breast
      Flowers to the sun
      And our little boat of life
Sets sail on the sea where it will sink

Holy ghost gods and goddesses
Dream dance dissolve
The universe evolves we

Only open ever out
Who refuses to give up the ghost
Though gone to ash and dust
All the live long day
Wild-winged wishbone play
Of thought and dream
Ever wrought in the light of day
Dark places where shadows feed on themselves
But we are of the earth, will sink back to her soil
Food for the great worm
Sustenance sucked from root to tree

In the gapping jaw, in the teeth of vision
You can't tell who's eating who even
On a day like this look up
And see forever beyond the blue-white distance
Wispy clouds disappear blown by the breath
Behind the teeth continuing to chew you
Until the void retches, spews you out empty
See what is in front of we

*Holy ghost gods and goddesses*
*come before your eyes*
*the old gods, long gone*
*glad to see you again*
*glad to see you*

*The ghost bones call*
*talk dry as chalk*
*chew you with vision teeth*
*with newly moistened mouth*

*The ghost bones call*
*to summon spirits*
*to sing seizing songs*
*to hold the soul by its body*
*to hold with healing hands*
*the pierced heart by its hooks*
*look inward*
*an open door*
*at the core*

*Pain is Permanent*

*Bliss is Forever*

# CLEOPATRA DREAMING

The young god sleeps in a coffin, a perfect fit
    The child sleeps in fire
The dove flies round the feathery tamarisk
    Pillar of the palace

Isis mounting her dead lover
As her barge gently rocks on eternity's river
Dead, down and dark he sends his seed

    Macedonian
Cleopatra-Pytolemy, Blood of Osiris

The great stacked stones, the pyramids
Perfectly designed, precisely positioned
3,000 years old when you were born Cleopatra
Born in the amniotic sack, born with a veil, sign of luck
The shroud of mystery, just one of the signs
Ishtar, Venus star, born between the horns of the moon
Daughter of Pharaoh, granddaughter of the Nile
    Isis on Earth
*Yes, your death was in the cup of your birth*
Your death where you choose snakes

Sunstruck, Egyptian music
Fainting, feels like floating
Belly dancers zill as they dance
Tiny bells and rattles sewn into costumes
Worn around ankle or wrists
Their rhythmic movement is the music
    Of the dance

Cleopatra, down adrift in dream
I saw you there in death
Three times they tried to assassinate you
        Little princess
Born under the augury of destruction
Human-headed-lion-hearted-cobra-hooded-sphinx

But you live still in man's memory
Here in my mind, dream realms
Legend, fable, myth, collide
Homemade history, techno-color mystery
Moves on the walls of change
A little girl, a queen unfurled
Rolled out of a rug
Springs up at the feet of Caesar

Wearing a navel ring from which hangs
A tiny golden bell, wearing a fishnet dress
        One bare breast
Soon you will wear Pharaohs beard
And the cobra crown
Soon you will bear Cesar a son
Cesar, deified, rose petals and laughter
Ides of March, knives of the Senate, snake bit
The son of Cesar and Cleopatra, Egypt and Rome
Too powerful to live

White kitten of the black cat
Granddaughter of the Nile
You chose snakes, sacred asps of Egypt
As high priestess you had danced
Since childhood with royal snakes
Well-fed serpents, full, slow-moving

After the sacrifice they liked the dance
Sensuous, twined round, supple strength
They gave tiny love bites, just enough toxins
To send you whirling in hallucinogenic trance dance

But tonight you offer up yourself for feast,
        You the sacrifice
You will feed the serpents, serve the soil
The soft ways are plenty, the easy outs
The potions and the poisons at hand
Assassination a royal art form
But you chose to dance with hungry asps

An irresistible surge, flowering fever
The immortal making
Golden fingernails of Egypt's dead
You chose your death, you who are who you are
The cup of your death was in your birth
Isis on Earth, Granddaughter of the Nile

Asps ancient of Egypt
Asps anxious for blood of the Nile
        In your veins, water of life
Now you are buried among the living stones
Where all your relatives dance and breathe in your bones

# THREE WORLDS WITHOUT FIRE

Geese flirt on the fly
Mate on water
Nest in down lined sand pits

Three worlds without fire

Migrating geese speak for the Goddess
Carry Her safe in the down of their breast
Monks in bright red hats, hands full of beads
Interpret their songs
       Channel the revelations into
       Good crops and spirit flight

Prayers rise on wings, on spinning wheels
       Paramahansa
The long necked gander
High above the earth
Among flocks of barking geese
       Howling with joy
Blue Sky goddess of Tibet
Has lapis lazuli hair

Gods along the silk road
       Ride kites
The spirits on a road of rope
Woven of red silk and sinew

Exchanging stories
        Ragged, rugged
Riding the winds on the rooftops
        Of the world

Below on the earth
        Eggs incubate
No veil between nature and the spirit world
Conches, long Tibetan horns and small bells
Spells, stupas, prayer flags
        Mantra's and demon masks

Migrating geese carry the goddess
Safe in the down of their breast
Flirt on the fly, mate on the water
Nest in down-lined sandpits
Three worlds without fire…

# AWAY FROM THE WORLD WOMAN

    In dreams
away from the world-woman
spins her top on the table
spins into open skies a fable
       wheeling away

Whirlpool Woman in the great lake of night
standing there in thigh-high waters
shoulder high reeds
there beneath the anthill huts
she pours milk over her head-she prays
not all clouds bring rain--she says.

She comes up out of there
wet with warmth & weather
She comes up out of there
      New Now
goes to the spirits' crossroad beneath the burial tree
where bodies bound in bright cloth hang from branches.
      She stops, stoops, takes her spoon and digs a hole.
      There at the crossroad
      she buries the shadows, plants them deep
      beneath earth touching prayer
      beneath water pouring prayer
      under hungry rocks and singing stones
      beneath air breathing prayer
      and fire burning prayer.

There she plants the shadows
buries yesterday
today is

Born

Where blue smoke holds up the sky
mystery lives, lends her eyes
in darkness, second sight.
Where the empty air is busy
with ghosts of the everyday dead
Ancestors enter her dreams
watch over her, sing in her dreams.


In dreams she drifts back
before she was born.
Her grandmother sees her coming
leaves off working in her garden
smiles her tangled tooth grin
begins to hum her old lullaby
takes great care there
prepares food for her soul.

She pitches her tent on dark clouds
drifts, dreams, awakes, standing in the lake

Night-girl,
nucleus and navel of the universe
Waterwalker, mud-foot,
umbilically rooted in earth.

She comes up out of there
an answer to prayer.
dripping warmth and weather
She comes up out of there.
      A fable wheeling away

Whirlpool Woman in the great lake of night

# CRUSHED & CRUCIFIED

Here caught in a snare of flesh and bone
Here her lair of lust, death and dust
Crushed and crucified by the transaxle
Of a truck, descending in death dreams
Drift with the shades
Feeding on their own shadows
Skull crushed and swollen beyond recognition
Blood and brain fluids, pour from eyes, ears, nose

Body broken to knowledge, pain
Bones of the spirit crushed to dust
To be born by the wind

I am wounded and weak
You should know as I speak
My feet are dust
Worms squirm in the mud filled
Fissures of my heart
I'm the walking wounded the weak link
Stumble knocked kneed, blind
Drunk-on-self down desires
My voice from a choked throat
Thru chattering teeth
Strong with the power of pain
This moment my mind shines
Sings the joy of Being

Growing to the grave
Still a glint in me glance
Teeth rotting gums
Sore breath growing older
Still the whispered words
Barely heard
Send chills
Fills me, spills over

Life's real pain and sorrow
Soaks some up
Lifts a little weight
A feather
Against the rock pile of realities

I'm wounded and weak
You should know as I speak
My feet are dust

The wilderness stares from everywhere
        Fierce eyes
With pounding heart I breathe deep
Try to return their glance without fear
Even iridescent salmon in the creek
Have shark's teeth, death's eyes to my surprise
My heart suddenly welcomes my wounds
My broken back, crushed skull, chronic pain
I am the lightning struck snag dying
Producing new growth

To enter the wound, within the wound
The world whirls or comes to a stop
In the heat and heart of my pain
Unable to move, mute chattering lips
Open empty mouths
Sing senseless songs in silence

I don't know who I am
Who am I
Who am I now
I AM

Up Jacobs ladder to wrestle Angels
Wings wide to encompass
To enclose the whole sky
To hear the Bloody cry
The song of rapture

The wounded healer
All my relations
All my relatives
Hold a mirror to the soul
See the Hole
Know the Whole heals
Move in a sacred manner

And Grace

Has a better chance of finding you

# THAT IS ME

Riding the Shamans drum
To lie in the eagles nest
The beast keeps growing
Backbone stretches, reaches heaven
Body expands, encloses sky
Stars nest in branches of my rib-cage

I'm growing so fast

Tall torso, my head lies at my feet
Composting the roots of the tree
That is Me

# LONG HOUSE HOME

Out of the long house home pitchfork loam
    Flowering pistil & stamen
Pollen of sun, shadow & shade unafraid
    Children singing
Of an archaic ordeal
Revealed in the unseeded soul…

Tarantula and rain in the candlelight & chronic pain
    Crumbled in a corner
Black & white & grey & run for the water waves
Run for the ruin & rave, some understand completely, wild
Connected to tides like doves in the sky, galloping stars
    Leaping light & alive…

The pain is the pain of fleeting joy
Flirting with quirky chaos is more interesting than
    Laying low & acting dumb
All stars beat the drum, compete for control
    While I dream you, old friend
Revealing the mystical concrete body of chronic pain
    In high-rise animal laughter.

    Sitting on granite, leaning on oak
Loving every day know the pain ain't going away
    Still laughing at the cosmic joke
    Beast of burden, bag of bones
    Face streaked with tears
    Tingling flesh & shivering spine

The body has a mind--of its own

Mammal machinery, muscle and meat
Keep the beat, fan the heat in the blood
     Feet of clay make mask of mud
Make feast of famine, make fast of sackcloth and ash
The actual flimsy flesh, time makes fine wine
     Makes grapes for the grail

Yellow-eyed owl screeching tires
Crawling in sewers grateful for reality
In cavernous dark the light
     Dreamtime
Painted caves, bedtime stories
     Bare arms raised in praise
     Mimes, magic, little cinemas
Language to bring the inner world out
     Connect us in knots of knowing

In soothing dark light sight unseen
     Between the labyrinth and ladder

     *Wake the God that sleeps in the wracked body*
     *Wait for the animal that chooses you*

     *Love the body you're living in...*

# ON & ON IT GOES

Flying out of time into eternity
Out past galaxies, unseen unknown
Racing with the Gods in Chariots of Fire
A blaze across the sky
Fire consuming all, burns a hole though my eyes
Eyes that see pain and sorrow, laughter and joy
Where's it all end
What's this eternal light in my brain
It won't go away!

Did you see that UFO last night
On & on it goes, where it lands nobody knows
Alien people with baby eyes
Baby blues, tender touch
I love you oh so much

Sandhill cranes overhead
Foghorn on the ocean
Wind chimes, bells of the Saints
Making music carried on the breeze

Hey, where's my scary stuff!
I don't know
Seems to have been lost along the way
Baggage thrown from the plane
Chuck that one overboard

Lightning time, baby time
Fast time, slow time
Its all relative
All my relatives
All of you

Can't escape
From mom & dad, bro & sis
Don't even want to
So out of time
Out of touch

Fill 'er up please

# ENTANGLEMENTS

**SHE**

*...I feel her presence in the common day*
*In that slow dark that widens every eye*
*She moves as water moves, and comes to me*
*Stayed by what was, and pulled by what would be...*

Theodore Roethke

# HE & SHE

An extraordinary meeting as hummingbird hovered
exchanging life with manzanita blossoms,
hum hum hummingbird
…dance flight song are one.

Raven walks slowly, dramatically
around & round the mirror his wings out wide.
And Coyote, the singer
with his human heart and his dancing blanket
and that other joker Manitoba or Jackalope
the great horned hare
thumping out a rhythm with his lucky rabbit's foot
and yodeling spirit songs.

Water Woman, lady laughing love and Spider Woman
mother, spinner of nets of medicines of healing herbs and
poisons.

They talk of circles
Great hoops, loops, round world, fireball sun, spun silver moon.
Circles of the Sioux and Bantu, and Aztec ball games.

They talk of man
Who either adored the mother and ignored the father
or idolized the father and murdered the mother.

A God not dead but divorced
wearing a golden helmet, holding a silver sword
parading before a mirror of false praise, vain as Raven.

When anyone could see
that

He & She

Are a Thing.

# THE LEAP

You have to take the terrifying and fearful
First leap of love
The heroic surrender of self to the other
And the equally difficult deed
Of accepting the other into yourself

When you do it completely
A new composite person is born in each
For me, it happened fast and all at once
I pulled back in some sort of
Gasping and grasping attempt
To hold on to my old self
But the attraction was too strong
The life our bodies want to lead
Life in line with the inevitable

# ADVENTURE

I flew with the thunderbird
From flames took flight
Flew too with the monkey eagle
        All before
I met the real adventure of my life

    At a rest stop

# MYSTERY

Stepping deep into your steaming streams
Fistful of fire I splash
I bend and bow to lap your cold waters
I dive and die in your cold currents
Cold and hard to hold

Freedom no fear
Falling a falcon with folded wings

Commitment
The long body of our life together
Passion
The wisdom of our blood pulsing

Our souls' animated essence
Eros, Wild Orchids, Orgasms
Umbilical Love Root
Molecular Emotion

The time is now today
Here where lovers lay
Locked lips and loins

One-eyed, twin-hearted
A single embryo
Our salty souls' grow
And shed their seed
On our bare hearts' soil

This mystic meat sheds its skin
Begins new

My soulmate
My soul's meat and wine
My mind's wind chimes
We are in this moment

Eternal love

# BATHING IN OUR OWN HOT SPRINGS

Squatting hunkering, inhaling hot spring steam
Wiping warm mud all over our bodies
A rush of blood aroused body heat
Lips looser, larger, pupils of the eyes
      Dilated completely
Two black pits direct to the soul
Heart beats faster, muscles contract
Muscular contractions comfort
Release healing hormones

Mystery medicines
Primordial moist
Your fluids flow
Flood my drought-dry soul
Relaxed arousal
Lasting longing sexual silk on silk
We anoint the night with the oil &
      Slime of love
With our own warmth and weather

Water, dripping, streaming
Water falling, cascading over stone
Bathing in our own hot springs
Carnivorous juices, naked mud ooze
Scrawl cryptic signs on your body
      Central altar of the earth
Mud dripping, drying, caking, cracking
      Us cracking up

    *& back up*
To stand under the waterfall
      HAH!!
   Cold, cold steep creek
Dripping cliffs, rain rippled rock

Standing, steaming, shivering, shaking
Goosebumps and grin
Shimmer in a halo of mist and spray
Dressed in a living lattice work
Of lacy, leafy shadow and milky moonlight

You are beautiful
Soft, round, six months pregnant
Luminous with in-being radiance

Squatting, hunkering inhaling hot spring steam
Wiping warm mud all over our bodies
A rush of blood, aroused body heat
Fire, desire, burns away pain
And in the cool morning an everyday miracle
Renewed virginity in the innocence of passion

Wading, splashing, diving in the stream
Back out with a shout, baptism by deluge
    Reborn, not born again
Risen with new flame in the flesh

   A night of shared blessings
   Bathing in our own hot spring

# FROG GODDESS

*Long sleeping,*
*returns with the rain*
*water woman*
*Who fetches the golden ball from the bottom of the well*

*Night singer, night singer, croaking, soaking*
*sound all around*
*And in the morning mud & creek grasses*
*Along the stream bed*
*squatting legs spread wide*
*Long strands of pearls, long strings of eggs*
*little pearls*
*Frog Goddess bleeding golden fertility*

*Seeding the earth in color*
*the sky with light*

---

# LIQUID RELAXATION

When you open with liquid relaxation
Spine- rooted eruption, beating heart
Heart of song, grain of sand

Molten reformation reshape me
Flesh & earth
Bone & stone unturned

Blow your windy fire
Softly on my brain

I awake from waking life in dream
In gardens out of time
On long-legged thighs
Up ziggurat mountains
To touch the womb domed sky

Nebuli
To kiss your knees…Carried away
Among visions…of primitive angels
Manna bread out of Heaven

————— ∞ —————

# INTO THE DEPTHS

My spirit familiar is female,
My mystical experience
Often sparked by ecstatic sexual emotion.
Bare feet on a mountain meadow
Your fingers on my face
The warm wet weight of sighs
Eyes embrace
The subtle shifts
Between erotic and mystical love

High priestess of the ancient mysteries
Self- anointed by nature, called
Mistress of mystic moonshine
Soft as steel the real deal

Harlot of my heart- mother of my children
Unsealer of the secrets of my soul

The milk from her breast
Comes to me more intimate than nursing
Never turns bitter in the belly
Umbilically attached
Submerged
In her ambrosial, amniotic fluids
Eternity dissolves and the universe evolves

She, high priestess
By nature anointed, rituals and formulas
A woman wanton, sexual energy, ecstasy
Builds, boils, erupts from her in full flame that
Burns away pain

Always in the new of morning
She has the same child's eyes
The virgins healing heart
Radiates a halo's golden light

*Thru Woman*
*Man is born*

*Finding the goddess*
*The god in man awakes*

# TWO-GETHER

Two-gether alone
Below deck, below the waves
Listening through the wooden hull
To the love calls of unseen whales
Inhaling their music like medicine
Oceanic, orgasmic
Or
Two sea battered seals
Sunning on a craggy shore
Two souls
Tossed by chance together
Or
Led by our hearts
Secret chartings
Down every road
To this meeting, this twining
Of flesh and spirit

Exchanging energies
Changing identities back and forth
You in the skin of my spirit
I whole in your soul
Twined bodies, intermingled minds
Home each in the other
The way well worn
Even the down dark places
Are lit with a moonlight brilliance
When we slow to mingle our souls
When we're alone,
Naked beyond time

Summers night stars come
Down to the ground
Surround us like fireflies

Trading eyes
Looking thru your eyes
At myself in you
Magnetism so strong, pull us apart, let go
We fly back together again dancing
Gravity so strong
It bends
Curves the space around you
Draws me pulls me in
Like a black hole
Sucks up suns

# SOULS

Men may have souls, invisible
Or a man's soul may rest and nest in his head
But the mortal goddess born of woman
Who knows Her own wilderness
Her spirit is warm, welcoming flesh
Woman's soul beats the drum of the heart
Pounds out the pulsing rhythms in rivers of blood
Lightning thru faint blue veins, thunder in her throat
Her soul is flesh and seeded Earth
Her spirit is pulsing wine, red blood and flowing milk
Rooted in earth, anchored in the calm harbor

Hair dances in the wind—

# I DREAMED OF YOU LAST NIGHT

I dreamed last night you nursed me
Held my man's body

Folded in your arms
An infant in a six-foot frame

Your nipples large
Each white drop of milk
Filled with the fluids of life

A joyful spring
Welling up in my spirit's dark cave

Where dreams of you fertilize my heart at dawn

# RAINSTICK

Within the rainstick, within the rainstruck cabin
Thunder, lightning, delight, rites, rituals, wild weather
Winter woods wail, trees tremble, leaves rustle
Raging winds wake the wilderness within
Awake, wildly awake, lightning lit electric

Within the rainstick, within the rainstruck cabin
Thunder right above, lightning from within the hard rain
Rain on the roof, darkness night
Rain on the roof, rhythm of the soul
Rain on the roof, blood of life on earth
Flowing down on thirsty soil

In the eye of the storm
In the womb of our one room cabin
Hand-built, hammer and saw
       Me and ma hover
     Now inches above the bed
      Takes up half the room
    Eye to eye      breath to breath
Brilliant gold light from a single kerosene lamp
Faint sighs, low windy moans, cabin groans
Creaking roof, sudden crack, thunder clap lightning
      One luminous being

    Embracing

Stab my heart with your tongue
Plunge deep, I melt, plunge deeper
Your torch tongue acetylene arcs

Friction of two souls' sparks
      Lightning licks
In the heat and quickening beat of two hearts
Meat is the myth that cooks on the fires of sex
Stab me through the heart with your tongue
Alchemy, mystery
      We become one
Spirit animal, growls, groans, moans
Speaks in tongues, in tongues

Brushstrokes painting paradise
Rippling, running rivers of living sap

And sweet sweat waters the need
The root-twined bodies need
To hold and caress, caress
Yes the language of love

Within the rainstick, within the rainstruck cabin
The mountains speak with the banshee voice of the storm
Thunder rolls, roars, shakes our tiny shack
Rain, hard rain pounds down on the roof
Rain bent sidewise by the wind
Whips walls and windows
The rainstick rhythm of the soul
Winter woods wail, trees tremble, leaves rustle
Raging winds wake the wilderness within
Awake, wildly awake, lightning lit electric
      Within the rainstick, within the rainstruck cabin

The hard rain is over, a light mist fills air
Full of the after rain aroma of the thickly
Forested mountains, a northerly breeze

Breath of God

Sweet and wet in my lungs and on my tongue
The sun comes and goes among the breaking clouds
Kaleidoscope of changing color and shade

Darkening greens suddenly flood with gold light
Shimmering diamonds in gold green hair
Sparkles alive, slow gems drip from each leaf
And roll more rapidly along pine needles
Reflects running rainbows in every drip

p
i
n
g          drop

The mountain speaks in silent pauses


Keeping still mountain
Sitting above rain-fresh-wet-woods
Glows in the rays of rising sun
Running down the mountain side
        Brooding, gurgling dark waters
Cascade down the canyon
        To the gorge below
Raindrops drip from trees

In the first light of day
A mist lifts up from the ground
And covers the earth
Later the sun will burn this mist
        Lift the veil

But now we caress
Unseen dampness
        Bare feet
        Trembling toes
Dig deep into the earth

        Hum along softly
        With the rest of Creation

# I ONLY...

I only wish
to touch your face with my fingers
to hold your earlobes
between my lips a moment
to pass a word eye to eye

The gift
the glint in your glance
to lay close together in the deep dark
to inhale your warm wet breath
Your being in the dark silence
absolute

Your presence
we turn
cuddle, fetal position, spoon-like
me wrapped around you
just touching

Drifting toward dream

# YOU DO THAT FOR ME

When I look in your eyes
You are always there
Splendor, pleasure
And new eyes for today's treasure
Like it's all happening for the first time
Only you do that for me

You wear the same short skirt
The same body you wore
More than twenty years ago
Your sky-blue-sea-grey eyes
Where I love to swim

Your eyes turned by dream
Fire agate burnt brown
Constantly changing colors
Still sing the same soft something
Shaking my soul's foundation
Yet the same dark passion
And bright innocence

In the silent savage soul
Golden bells toll

Only you do that
For me

## JUMP FROM ETERNITY

Angel exchanges eternity for a woman
Trades eternity, wings and armor

Roaring silence or meaningless noise
The angel fell headlong from heaven's bell
Jumped, wearing armor & crossed wings
Jumped from its black and white haven
To the hard concrete world of color

Would have been crushed on gravity's anvil
But caught in the cotton soft arms of the child
Who simply smiled at the fallen angel

His wings feel the fastest free-fall of all
The wild fast free fall, the long moment
The light speed stop of time

*Angel angel falling*
*I hear you sing, hear you calling*
*Unfurl your wings and stop your drop*

His wings flapping furiously to slow his descent
Created a whirlwind of rising dust and warm air

A few people turned
Glanced briefly in his direction
Their eyes too focused
On this world only

They saw a man with hair blowing in the wind
Wings luminous, shimmering, barely visible

Gnostics believe each soul has a perfect mate
They merge and make one angel
In the spin of vision the two souls
Ying and yang make one God
Holding all between them

Caress the vast void
As to space as space is to sky
Separated in times place

# WALKING ON GIA

## THE DIMENSIONS OF THE MORNING

*Furtively sounding*
*In the high*
*Halls of God, the voice which is*
*Life begins to sing.*
*You will listen O you will not be afraid*
*To listen…*
*All these do*
*The wolf, the fengy, the bear, the wide*
*Fish; and deer, the silky rat, the snail,*
*The onises—even the goat*
*That waves his funny tail at trains*
*Is listening.*
*Do you now faintly*
*Hear the voice of life?...*

*…The voice which is life*
*Shall sound over all the earth,*
*And over all who lie deep*
*In its green arms-- …*

Kenneth Patchen

# HAWK GLIDES THRU BLUE TIME

Hawk glides through blue time
It's shadow moves across
Burnt-gold-cougar-colored-hills
Where a lone lion lopes and soundlessly
Leaps a bob-wire fence
No change in speed or direction
Fluid muscles, liquid motion
A short sidelong glance, eye contact
-An electric spasm up my spine-
A lone lion leaps a barbwire fence
Disappears in the tree line

Snags, driftwood
Walking on fallen logs
Happy for gurgling water

     Stop

Look deep, undulant flowing
Silky soft and sinewy muscle
Of rippling rock, ridges running
Along the granite river bed
Below the water, deep calm pool
Trout, iridescent rainbow
Darts in and out of an underwater cave

Pale soft golden glow
Waning moon sagging low
Over Blue Mountain
Sounds of running water
And sounds of Chinese opera singers
In the wondrous wildly odd
Bird-bark, cat-squawk songs
Of a far away fox
And
Coyote angels sing
Windy gospels
In back country gorges
Wild windy gospels
In back country gorges

Wingbeat of horned owl
Overheard, overhead
The feathered air large with life
Eyes follow ears
Fly in the heat of the moon
Find the owl, gliding low and slow
Through moonlight and shadow
Disappearing in dark woods

Waves wash and lap the shore
Light breeze breaks over the embers
Dim coals glow red and spark in the dark
Up above the charcoal and pin-prick cinders
    Of the night sky

"Stars teach endless mind"
The waters are quiet
The air is still
The rocks and
Mountains
Flowing

# BUMP ON A STUMP

Sitting on a stump
   listening to wind
      singing in pines

Eternity whittled down like this
   Chain-sawed stump
      hours and minutes
         board feet and woodchips

High billowy clouds blue-sky
   no Babylon below, no cities
      selling sea water to quench your thirst
         to salty dog your dollar

The buck shucks his antlers
   and leaves them for me
      on this spot where I stop
         and sit, bump on a stump


On the path up here a snake skin recently shed
   Larvae Transformations, the moon
      the cocoon ruptures, rips, opens…
         the souls shell cracks from the inside out

      Release

         an iron-beaked bird beats its wings

         lifts slowly from the giant knotted pine

# SPRING MORNING

When I run with the sun as it rises
in the morning, sucking the last
juices from the dew drenched
honey sweet manzanita blossoms
*Alive*
When I dart suddenly off the dirt road
and sprint full speed across the meadow
thru dew-hung lupine, fire-lit by the sun
straight at the grazing deer
*All alive*


Winter Afternoon


Coming home, Blue Mountain
darkening clouds thick fog
the tree ten feet away
just a shadow
and the mountain the steep cliffs
just beyond unseen

suddenly the old bridge
the river, the waterfall
a few brush strokes like
a Chinese landscape


Cross the bridge, disappear in the fog bank
thru the mist into the meadow
two deer on the far side

I walk a few steps
stop and stand awhile

When I move again they break and run
in a quick sprint I chase after them
into the tree line and back up a trail

Blue jay flys low overhead
and out of sight
the run is fun the deer are gone
I'm almost Home

# MIMOSA MYSTERY'S

The large-limbed mimosa creaks in the wind
    cotton candy colored blossoms
    sweet-heavy-honey-dew-aroma

The old tree plays host to a bunch of bees
    bumble bees, honeybees, meat bees
    and a dozen or more humming birds

Some of the birds take a break from their feast
    sit perched on branches, chattering
    most remain at work, wings hum

Dive bomb blossoms, dip beaks deep
    dripping nectar, the continuous drone
    buzzing bees and hummingbirds

Their motion, the music, nature, bull-roaring
    drones, drowns out *everything*
    a sense of wheeling, feeling weightless

Not flight, but lifted up, carried out, *beyond a moment*
    and I'm back on hands and knees
    beneath the budding mimosa tree


At the place where my yard gives way to the wilderness
    a clump of green Manzanita
    and bare grey whitethorn bush
    in the spring **they** hosted the great feasts

Mistletoe, golden bough, death's crown tops the old oak snag
      that stands still ashen white & quicksilver grey
      The sway of green hills, pine boughs wave in wind

Sundrops behind cardboard hills, peach-pink sky
      the same hue as the mimosa blossoms
      colors begin to fade as the night comes on

      Goats drift thru darkening green grass
        the windmill is still, standing a ladder
          to the crescent moon and Venus star

# HIGH MOUNTAIN THICKET

A high mountain thicket
A grove paved with golden leaves
Dark blue shadows swim with amber light

Wind wakes in pines
Stirs in oak leaves
Moves on the water

The shimmering of sunlight
Reflected off the creek
Onto the platinum aspen

At this place
In this moment
Play of sunshine and shade
Swirling water and whirlpools
'reflected sunlit leaves
Move in gentle wind
The motion of mystery itself

Lay listen
Wind whistles
Leaves rustle
Lay belly down in the grass
Head turned to the side
Eyes focus un-focus     re-focus
On this wet tissue thin monument

This fallen petal
Lit illuminated
By reflected & filtered sunlight

Lay listen

   the wind whispers

      wails

        becomes silent

# ...AND JUST BEYOND THAT

Climbing the small twisted
      Tree, tallest point in these
Mountains, wind swept, sun-weathered
      Laying hours in muscled limbs
Birds nesting in leaf-hair

A few billowing clouds
Drift by a crescent moon
In the day-blue sky

The shadows of the clouds
Roam the valley below
Dark dinosaurs that
Disappear as the sky clears

Sierra (saw-toothed), distant jagged
      Dragon teeth peaks
Grin in purple majesty

And just beyond that...

# GUST OF SPARROWS

A gust of sparrows rises and cuts across
The apricot cream and blood-red clouds
      Just above the set sun
Indian paintbrush shooting stars & buttercups
      In a windy green dance
      The barefoot meadow
      Jagged peaks all round
Séance of touch, feet meet earth
And tell as much as smell, sight or sound

      In the night
The grove of ghostly white snags
All bent by the prevailing winds to face northwest
Their empty limbs sag down supplicant

      Hanging from each branch
Thousands of thin white twigs create
      Spider lace fingers
The great grey snags sway in forever wind

A Temple of standing stooping skeletons
In the light of a full moon
A quite choir of ghost snags and wind
Teach the beauty of death and decay
Full of life; termites, ants, insects of every kind
Families of woodpeckers, squirrels, owls & others
Slowly rotting they become part of this

Rich soil, receive seed, start over

# TEA LEAVES & OTHER ORACLES

Cloudmaker in the southwest at sunset

Peach colored puffs
Drift slowly
On prevailing winds
Cumulus
Calligraphy of crashing clouds

Shapeshifting, storytelling…

And up above
Slow motion
Cirrus clouds climb
The highest reaches
Of earths atmosphere
      Spread
           Thin
                Dissolve
In arcane symbols and signs
Legible as tea leaves

Every gnarled and wrinkled old snag
Has many stories to tell

And every stump is riddled with mystic runes

Rings of the stump
Time telling runes

Walking on river of rocks
Drought dry
Stepping stone to stone
Rocks scattered
Along this sandy bed
Runes to be read

A Zen garden recently raked

    by the Mother of Masters

# LOVE FEAST

Nature's love feast
of praying mantis & black widow
      *gotta have it hunger*
erotic courtship dance of cranes
lifelong love of the wolf
      dove thought realms
      bird-feather poems
      insects as individuals
mammal religion, amphibian religion
flight of bird, dive of dolphin
the same religion as trees and stones

each insect egg is intricate
      and unique
caterpillars' have tubular hearts
the dance language of honeybees
      elaborate and precise
monarch butterflies fly thousands of miles
      to mate and breed

After mating in the air
honeybees leave their penis
in the Queen bee
rip it off after sex
sealing their seed inside
ensuring the next generation
they fall to the earth
      and die

Deep breathing trees
oxygenate the air
placenta, the buried after- birth
fruit trees in bloom
rising sap, soil rooted plants
feasting on earth, air, sun and water

Insect eating heliotropic plants
petals form a smooth cup
sweet bait an insect falls into
the flower folds in on itself
        consumes its prey


Winged fish flying
siren sea singing from the river's mouth
        at the ocean's edge
salmon fight their way upstream
        spawn and die
frigate birds dive for their dinner
mammals give live birth
nurse their young
dream dolphins playful
        in the Big Blue

        Nature
*mother* of the love feast
of praying mantis & black widow
*gotta have it hunger*
erotic courtship dance of cranes
life long love of the wolf

*all pollens bless*
*the now born child*
*every funeral*
*a festival*
*and feast*

# IF

     If
words & wishes
were enough to heal
all wounds

     If
will and work
would fill
every need
And all hope
held hard
to the heart's heat

     If…

---

# NEW MOON

The black moon an empty husk
The new moon is black
The wisdom of the soul lies in what −is−
No moon, fading stars, flickering fireflies
Dawn comes on
       earth altar
       sacred stones

The soul must face embrace death
Memory wide & deep contains the past
What is possible incubates
        is born from what is *present*

# GRIEF IS REAL IS RELEASE IS HEALING

Made in the USA
San Bernardino, CA
27 September 2014